Dedication

This book is for my friend, Carol Kyryliuk, who makes "character education" the focus of her teaching and who demonstrates integrity and compassion in the classroom of life.

Teach me, O Lord, to follow your decrees; then I will keep them to the end. Give me understanding, and I will keep your law and obey it with all my heart. (Psalm 119:33–34)

Acknowledgements

Special thanks to Janie Schmidt and Kathy Zaun of Grace Publications and to Donna Borst, who has been a constant supporter of my "stories." I would also like to acknowledge the work of Dr. Philip Fitch Vincent and his colleagues at the Character Education Group for their inspirational efforts in the work of using literature to teach core values in schools.

Special Note to Teachers

The method of "teaching by story" has become a popular and fashionable form of pedagogy, but for Christian educators, it is a natural and comfortable mode of teaching. With the example of Jesus Christ, the "best" storyteller ever, we have good reason to choose stories as our vehicle for delivering larger, more complex messages. Stories, especially those in which children are the protagonists, give youngsters an opportunity to think about important, sometimes challenging, issues. The stories and enrichment activities featured in this book can be used in language arts, social studies, or in Bible study lessons. The stories can also be "worked in" to the day or shared with parents at home. *Developing Character in Christian Kids* is not designed to be a separate strand of the curriculum. Instead, this book offers a simple, refreshing way for children, parents, and teachers to explore some tough issues and to gain insight into how character is built and tested, daily and through experiences in the real world.

Introduction

Talking with children is often the most natural and effective way of "teaching" important ideas. Stories, conversations, discussions, debates, and simple "chats" about critical ideas give children the opportunity to share their own experiences and to get inside the minds of their teachers. The stories that we choose and use in the classroom give children much to think about.

Developing Character in Christian Kids provides teachers with a unique way to infuse "character education" into the classroom. It consists of six stories that can be read to the children to help them develop such valuable character traits as developing a work ethic, respecting others, being kind, being good citizens and servants, having integrity, being responsible, and being compassionate. Following each story are teacher resource pages offering activities that will help children develop valuable skills in these areas: language arts, literacy, critical thinking, following directions, character development, math, and more. Choose some or all of these activities to do with the children. (Any necessary reproducible activity pages are included as well.)

An **appendix** is included in the back of the book and contains a **letter to parents**, **ideas for building community support for character education**, and a **checklist** to be used to evaluate each child's character development as he or she works through this book. The letter to parents explains the objectives of this book and the importance of character development. Send it home to parents before beginning. The ideas for building community support for character education provides a list of ways others in the community can try to help children develop positive character traits. The checklist is a guideline you can use to help you determine each child's development of the six values featured in the book.

The stories in this book are a wonderful way to enhance character development as they present children in "real-life" settings in which their Christian values may be tested or may conflict with what others believe. These stories tell about children who develop, test, and try out their values and then find that God's ways are the best ways. They depict children living their faith in a challenging world. The accompanying activities are designed to be integrated into the curriculum so that basic skills and concepts can be taught through the character-rich stories. *Developing Character in Christian Kids* uses humor, real-life situations, and child-centered stories to make values meaningful.

The Egg Roll Empire
A Story About Developing a Work Ethic

by Dr. Linda Karges-Bone

Bible Verse to Learn: *Turn my heart toward your statutes and not toward selfish gain.* (Psalm 119:36)

"Not too thin, not too thin. The filling will spill out, and it will be a waste. Not good. Not good!" Grandmother Wong's voice gently nudged her eight-year-old granddaughter, Karen. At the long, white enamel table, Karen and her grandmother stood rolling out wraps for egg rolls. Over and over again, Karen practiced her skill. "It is right to do things right," Grandmother Wong had said many times. Making egg rolls was not easy, especially for an eight-year-old who would rather be out in-line skating than egg roll rolling.

Karen giggled at the thought! In-line skating instead of egg roll rolling—it was a pun. What fun! She giggled again.

"What's so funny?" demanded Grandma Wong.

"Nothing Grandma," Karen respectfully replied. Funny or not, it was not good to be disrespectful to one's elders. And Grandma Wong was certainly old. She was over 60 years old. Yet she and Grandpa Wong had been the owners of the Egg Roll Empire restaurant for 20 years, ever since they had come to America from mainland China. Grandma Wong believed in working hard. "Not to hardly work. Work hard," she would say. Everyone in Karen Wong's family worked at the Egg Roll Empire—her grandparents, of course, and her mother, her father, her two older brothers, their wives, and now, Karen, too.

Karen kept rolling out egg roll wraps. Meanwhile, Grandmother Wong had disappeared into the deep freezer to bring out some pink shrimp to mix into the egg roll filling. Karen took a moment to rest and think. She was tired of working every afternoon after school, and now summer was coming. "I'll be working all summer," thought Karen, and she was a little bit sad. "I wish I was like Rochelle. She has so much time to herself."

The Egg Roll . . . continued

Suddenly, Karen heard a cheerful voice coming through the kitchen. "Karen, are you back here?" It was Rochelle.

"Come on back. I'm egg rolling. Again," sighed Karen. Rochelle appeared at the table. Her black hair was tightly corn-rowed and capped with yellow and blue beads. Rochelle's mom was a cosmetologist, "somebody who fixes other people's hair, you know," as Rochelle proudly told her. Naturally, she took great care with her little girl's hair.

"Can I stay over here for a while?" asked Rochelle hopefully. "Mama is working late at the shop. There's a big wedding at the church tomorrow, and Mama is doing the hair on six bridesmaids. They all needed late appointments because they work late in the city. You know." Rochelle liked to add "you know" to many of her sentences; she liked the way it sounded.

Grandmother Wong answered, "Stay, stay. You can wrap these silverware. Wrap them good in napkins. But wash your hands first. Hot water and soap. Move fast little girl. Not to waste time." It was Friday night, their busy night. Many people ordered in on the telephone or stopped by after work to pick up Friday night dinner from the Egg Roll Empire.

"Do you mind working?" Karen whispered to Rochelle as they bundled silverware into napkins. Grandmother Wong had scooped up the egg rolls to take them to Karen's father who skillfully dipped them into a deep fryer full of peanut oil.

"It is nice here," said Rochelle. "I like to help. Besides, your family is so much fun to be around. I like the way you take care of each other and the way that you pray together before every meal."

"Fun?" asked Karen. "All we do is work. Every day, after school, that is, after I do my homework and studies, I come back here and work. That's no fun."

"We go to 'Girls Alive' at the church on Wednesdays," Rochelle reminded her, "and we went to the movies last Sunday afternoon."

The Egg Roll . . . continued

"I guess so," sighed Karen. "But with summer coming, I'll be here working even more. Everybody else will be having fun, and I'll be slaving away at the Egg Roll Empire."

"I wish I could work here this summer," said Rochelle. "Mama's going to put in a lot of hours at the shop this summer. She and her friend Louise are saving all the money they can to put a down payment on their own salon, you know. I can't hang around over there because of the customers. Mama says they come in to relax and not to watch somebody's children. I'll be by myself at the apartment. Babysitters cost too much, you know."

Karen thought about what Rochelle had said. Still, it sounded like an adventure, being by yourself at the apartment. You could do whatever you wanted to and nobody was around to say, "Work harder, not hardly work!"

A few days later, the girls arrived at the Egg Roll Empire with their report cards in hand. Karen's grandfather examined their report cards carefully for good marks. He gave Karen and Rochelle a dollar for every "A" that they earned. Rochelle's grandfather lived far away, so he had "adopted" Rochelle as part of the family. Between the two girls, they had nine dollars.

"What shall we do with it?" Karen asked eagerly. They were eating bowls of steaming soup with egg cooked into it. "Egg feeds the brain. Get smarter," Grandmother Wong would say every day as she poured out the broth.

"I'm going to save part of mine, you know, for a rainy day," said Rochelle, "and then I'm going to buy a new book in the Mystery Girls series. I've already got 14 of them."

"I read all the time," said Karen. "I'm going to get my in-line skates out of layaway. Mother put them in layaway a month ago, and we have been paying some every week. With my money, there should be enough."

Later that evening, after the dinner rush was over, Karen and her mother drove over to Discount City and carefully counted out the money to get the speedy new skates out of layaway.

The Egg Roll ... continued

"I can hardly wait to try them," Karen bubbled. The next morning, Karen woke early and scooted out to the sidewalk to skate. She was surprised to see Grandmother Wong hurry out of their apartment across the hall. She was carrying a bag from Discount City.

"Wait. Wait child," called Grandmother Wong. "Put these on first. Not smart to break your head." She pulled a pink neon helmet and matching elbow and knee pads from the shopping bag.

"Grandmother, these are the coolest!" breathed Karen. "How did you know?"

"I have eyes. I see things," nodded Grandmother Wong.

"Thank you," said Karen, and she hugged her grandmother awkwardly, tilting on her new skates and padded with her new gear.

Karen skated for an hour. She dipped, swirled, and fell many times. Each time, the padding and helmet protected her. She couldn't help but think of her grandmother who worked so hard at the Egg Roll Empire to earn the money for these nice things.

Karen skated over to Rochelle's apartment building. Buzzing the intercom, Karen told her friend, "Come on down. It is eleven o'clock, time to set up the buffet for the lunch business."

"I don't believe it," Rochelle told her as she walked and Karen skated over to the restaurant. "I thought you hated having to work all summer. No fun, you know. What happened?"

"All those eggs, I guess," replied Karen, with a giggle. "My brain got fed, and I got smarter."

"Ah, my helpers," smiled Grandmother Wong as they entered the Egg Roll Empire. "Just in time for the lunch business. Good thinking. Time to work hard . . ."

"Not to hardly work," finished Rochelle and Karen. And so they did.

The Egg Roll Empire

Language Arts

1. Using a large sheet of chart paper and markers, create a chart story entitled "10 Good Things About Work." Sitting in a group around the chart paper, the children can brainstorm reasons why working is important and fun. Record their responses on the chart paper or let them write the answers themselves.

2. Read aloud the story "Whitewashing the Fence" from *Tom Sawyer* (by Mark Twain). Using the chalkboard, help the children make a list of similarities and differences between Karen's experiences and Tom Sawyer's experiences.

3. Instruct the children to write individual stories that begin with the story starter: *God honors honest work because . . .* The children can then illustrate the stories with pictures cut from newspapers or magazines, showing people at work.

4. Show the children how to use tape recorders and cassette tapes to tape "interviews" with grandparents or older adults from your church or neighborhood. The children can ask them if "working hard" means the same thing today as it did when they were younger. These interviews can then be written up as reports.

5. Find and duplicate a simple recipe for making egg rolls. Put the recipe on an overhead transparency and guide the children in reading the steps. Then the children can copy the recipe in their neatest handwriting on recipe cards and take them home. Use the reproducible recipe card found on page 10.

   (Note: This is a fun activity to do in conjunction with the egg roll making activity from Social Studies Activity 2 on page 8.)

6. Use the "Summer Reading List" on page 12 to help parents make the most of learning time during the summer months. Fill in the blank lines with titles of books that you recommend for the children's developmental levels.

Social Studies

1. Guide the children in locating mainland China on the world map. Then guide them in locating your city on the world map. Mark both places with a sticker pin. Connect the places with a string. Then help the children analyze a list of similarities and differences in the geography of both places. (Make page 13 into a transparency or use it as an individual student activity page in conjunction with this activity.)

The Egg Roll Empire

Social Studies continued

2. Invite a parent or volunteer who can prepare egg rolls to do so at your school, or perhaps the class can visit a Chinese restaurant to see them being made. It would be wonderful if each child could learn to roll out his or her own. The deep fryer, however, is a bad idea!

3. Discuss differences in cultures represented in your classroom. Use the chart on page 14 to facilitate your discussion. This chart can work nicely as a "paired activity" in which two children work together to complete their work. For more fun, have the children bring in foods from their cultures.

Math and Problem Solving

1. Using the string that was placed on the world map (Social Studies Activity 1 on page 7), have the children estimate the distance between mainland China and your city. They can write their guesses on the in-line skates pattern found on page 11. (This pattern can be reproduced and cut out prior to the lesson.) Be sure to put the children's names on their estimates and then display them on the board. Compare the estimates to the real distance.

2. Use the egg roll storyboard on the bottom of page 10 to play "Egg Roll Math." Reproduce the shrimp and vegetable pieces found on page 11 and let the children cut them out. The children can use the shrimp and vegetable "cutouts" to create multiplication and division problems to solve. The children can also practice number skills when you give them oral directions such as the following:

   a. If you want to make 6 egg rolls with 4 shrimp in each, write the multiplication equation to show this. ($6 \times 4 = 24$)

   b. If you want to plan an egg roll party for your class and you need 3 egg rolls for each student and teacher, how many will you need to fry? (Write the equation (_____ $\times$ 3 = _____) on the board and guide the children in solving for the right answer.)

3. Introduce money skills using "The Egg Roll Empire" story. The children can use play money to role-play Karen and Rochelle's gift of $9 for earning good marks. Pair children up and have them write their own "word problems" for spending the money.

The Egg Roll Empire

Character Education Enrichment

1. Discuss the concept of "work ethic" with the children. Invite them to discuss the questions below in small groups prior to Activity 2, "Ethics in Action."

   • *Why does working hard and honestly honor God?*

   • *Do you have to work in a "Christian" job, such as being a minister, to demonstrate how much you love God and want to serve him?*

   • *Can a person earn too much money?*

2. "Ethics in Action": Invite a panel of Christian adults (parents, church members, community leaders, etc.) to a juice and muffins breakfast followed by a panel discussion. The goal of this activity is to have the children ask the panel members questions about developing a work ethic and how this is part of their Christian walk. Let the children develop the questions as part of their earlier group discussions on "work ethic."

3. "Christians at Work" bulletin board: Start a current events board on which you can attach pictures or articles the children bring in about workers who also celebrate Christianity. Encourage them to look for politicians, athletes, artists, homemakers, and scientists who do not try to separate what they do from who they are in Christ.

4. "My Ideal Job" activity (page 15) serves as a critical skills task that ends this unit of instruction on a positive note. The children apply what they have learned from the story, "The Egg Roll Empire," and its corresponding activities to write about their ideal job.

Egg Roll Recipe Card

_____

_____

_____

_____

_____

_____

_____

_____

Egg Roll Math Storyboard

Egg Roll Math Cutouts

GP275702 Developing Character in Christian Kids

Summer Reading List

Reading during the summer can be an important "job" for children. They can work to develop their reading skills and gather new information and ideas.

The following list of books is appropriate for children in grade _____,

and the books can be found at the following places: _____

_____

_____

	Author	Title
Books About Families		
	_____	_____
	_____	_____
	_____	_____
	_____	_____
Books About New Places		
	_____	_____
	_____	_____
	_____	_____
	_____	_____
Books About Famous People		
	_____	_____
	_____	_____
	_____	_____
	_____	_____
Other		
	_____	_____
	_____	_____
	_____	_____
	_____	_____

Name _____

Geography Comparison Chart

China	_____ (state)
Ocean Borders	
Mountains in the Area	
Climate	
Temperature	
Landforms (hills, plains, valleys, rivers)	
Other	

Name _____

Cultures in Our Classroom

List the cultures represented in the classroom in the left-hand column. Be sure to include specific cultures. For example, Vietnamese children will have different experiences than Thai children. Don't assume all "Asian" groups are the same.

Culture	Language	Family Life	Foods	Church Traditions

Name _____

My Ideal Job

Write a job description of your "ideal job." Discuss what you would do each day and how you would honor God through the use of your talents and skills. Choose a Bible verse that would be your "guiding" principle for this ideal job.

Job Title _____

Bible Verse _____

_____

_____

Job Description _____

_____

_____

_____

_____

_____

_____

_____

_____

_____

_____

_____

_____

_____

_____

_____

I Am Really an Artist
A Story About Respecting Individual Differences

by Dr. Linda Karges-Bone

Bible Verse To Learn: *For God does not show favoritism.* (Romans 2:11)

Elena sat very straight in the blue kitchen chair. Tiny bits of silver wrapping paper covered the checked tablecloth and little shreds of silver paper sprinkled on the kitchen floor, but Elena kept cutting.

"Elena, would you like to try some of this chili that I am cooking?" asked her mother. "It's really spicy, the way you like it."

"No, thank you, Mama," Elena mumbled. She kept cutting the silver paper.

"I thought I had thrown that crumpled old paper in the trash," laughed her mother. "What a little scavenger you are!"

"What is a scavenger?" asked Elena. This time she looked up.

"Well little one. A scavenger is like a little mouse that hunts for any crumb left from the corn bread. It will fill its stomach with the leftovers that the broom misses," said her mother. She began to sweep the shiny, silver pieces of wrapping paper into a neat pile on the floor.

"Wait Mama, I need those for my picture. Besides, I'm not a scavenger. I am an artist! See those silver paper pieces? I'm going to glue them all over this black paper. Can you guess what my picture will be?" asked Elena.

"Let me see," smiled her mother. "It is a picture of the silver stars in the sky, isn't it?"

"No, Mama," giggled Elena. "Not stars. These are fireflies. Remember the fireflies that we saw at the window the other night?" asked Elena.

Her mother looked surprised. "Why little one, that was a long time ago. What made you think of it now?"

I Am ... an Artist continued

"I always think about things," began Elena. "I think and think. Then I find something pretty like the silver paper that was in the trash can. And then the fireflies jump onto my paper, right out of my head. I am a thinker and an artist," she finished.

"I think you must be," laughed her mother.

Elena went back to her artwork. Her mother remembered that a few days earlier, Elena had gathered a sandwich bag full of pine needles, leaves, moss, and acorns on her way home from school. Then she spread minty-smelling paste on a piece of paper and created a wonderful picture out of these things from nature by gluing them on in a pattern. It seemed that Elena could make art out of anything.

But the next day, Elena did not run in from the bus with acorns and leaves. She walked in slowly, and her small face looked sad.

"What happened, little one?" asked her mother. She put down her sewing and gathered Elena into her arms.

"This was not a good day for me," said Elena. "My teacher put a sad face on my math paper. She said that it was too messy."

Elena's mother looked at the math paper. She began to count out loud. "Two plus one is three. That one is right. Two plus two is four. That is correct. I do not understand this. Every problem is right," sighed her mother.

Then Elena's mother saw the flowers. A trailing vine of morning glories, a smiling yellow sunflower, and a purple pansy—all drawn with crayon around the sides of Elena's math paper. At the top of the page was a note that said: "Keep your paper neat. Too messy." There was a sad face drawn on top of the purple pansy.

"How did these flowers get on your math lesson?" asked her mother in a gentle voice.

I Am . . . an Artist continued

"Well, Mama, I finished the lesson before the others. Then I began to think about the flowers around the duck pond at the park. A picture came into my head, and pretty soon, it was all around the edges of my math paper. I'm sorry Mama," sighed Elena.

Elena's mother looked upset. She said, "The flowers are very good and so is the math lesson. I think that your teacher does not understand something."

"What?" asked Elena.

"You sit down and eat your cheese and crackers," ordered her mother. "Artists need lots of energy."

Then Mama picked up the telephone and pressed the buttons. In a minute, she said very politely, "Good afternoon, may I speak with Miss Greene, the kindergarten teacher? Please tell her that Elena's mother, Mrs. Gomez, would like to speak with her."

Elena's brown eyes grew wide.

"Hello, Miss Greene," began Elena's mother. "I was worried about the note and sad face on Elena's math paper. Elena's numbers were all correct and very neat. Why did you find the paper too messy?"

Mama listened and nodded.

"I see what you mean about the math, but the flowers were so beautiful. I think that you do not understand about Elena. When Elena gets a picture in her head, pretty soon the picture comes out, sometimes even on a math paper. So, would you mind if Elena brings her sketch book to school? Then if she finishes her work early, she will have a place to draw," said Elena's mother.

I Am . . . an Artist continued

Elena's mother listened again and smiled. "What a fine idea. I knew you would understand if we talked. I am sure Elena will be pleased. Thank you, Miss Greene," she said.

She hung up the phone and sat next to Elena.

"Miss Greene has a wonderful idea. She will put out colored chalk and markers and drawing paper for all the children to use when they finish their work. What do you think?"

"Oh, Mama," smiled Elena. "You mean I can be an artist at school and at home?"

"You are always an artist, Elena. It is part of the special person you are. God made you to be an artist. He planned this for you even before you were born," smiled her mother.

"How does God get such good ideas?" asked Elena. "Does he have a plan for every child?"

"Yes, he does," laughed her mother. "And it is a perfect plan, just like everything God makes. Every child is different, but it is all part of the plan."

"I guess God likes things to be different, so he won't get bored," thought Elena out loud.

"Maybe so," laughed her mother again. "And speaking of good ideas—what have you carved out of that cheese?"

"I noticed that this hunk of cheese looked sort of like a bird. So I took the butter knife and cut a bit, and the cheese became a bird. Just like that!" finished Elena.

"You are really amazing," said her mother.

"I am really an artist," said Elena.

"I believe that you really are," laughed her mother. And together, they gobbled up the hunk of cheese that was once a bird.

I Am Really an Artist

Language Arts

1. After reading the story aloud, ask children to respond verbally or in writing to the following prompt: *I am really . . .* Ask the children to consider how God's plan for their lives might include the use of their talents.

2. Guide the children in doing research to find out how talents and abilities make the world interesting. Show the children how to use a CD-ROM encyclopedia to research "Famous Women Artists." Working in teams, the children can find facts about the artists. They should include the following: name; birthdate; country of origin; style of art; preferred media; family information; interesting fact or quote from the artist. This information can be recorded on the board or on index cards. Encourage the children to use the computer to present the written material in an interesting, readable style.

3. Explain to the children that the way that one speaks and communicates is part of one's cultural background. To emphasize this point, help the children create an original dialogue (taped or written) between Elena's mother and her daughter's teacher. Ask the children these questions: *If Elena was Hispanic, how might her cultural background affect the story? How might your culture change the dialogue or the outcome of the story?*

4. Invite a Christian artist or writer to your classroom for a visit. Guide the children in preparing interview cards using a copy of page 23.

Creative Arts

1. Give each child a piece of construction paper to present an image of himself or herself as the person that he or she wrote about in Language Arts Activity 1. Let the children use crayons or markers to make the images colorful and detailed. Display these images in the classroom.

2. Give the children glitter, glue, markers, felt, scissors, a copy of page 24, and sheets of construction paper (black) they can use to design original nameplates. Invite them to design letters that attempt to express something interesting about their talents. For example, a child named Tara might use strong colors such as purple and red to depict a strong personality and could include images of pens and pencils to show her love of writing. When the children have finished their nameplates, have them cut them out and glue them to the black paper.

3. Give the children graph paper, rulers, and pencils to use to create a scale drawing of the ideal artist's studio. What kind of art do they specialize in? Where would they place windows? How much space would they need? What kind of lighting would be necessary? What kind of fixtures and furniture would be necessary? Have the children use the information gathered from their "Interview With an Artist" (page 23) to make this activity more authentic.

I Am Really an Artist

Science

1. Tell the children that artists often use color to express their ideas and feelings. Go to the library and check out some books on color. See if the children can help you answer these questions and then create a chart that demonstrates what they learned about light: *What is the relationship between color and light? What part of the brain senses color?*

2. Use the recipe below to make a strong soap bubble solution. Then let the children dip twisted pieces of wire into the solution. They will create a film of beautiful colors. But how did the colors emerge? Have the children find out by researching the term *interference.* It has to do with the way that light reflects from the inner or outer surfaces of the bubble. Let the children compare many shapes of bubbles.

   Directions for Making Bubble Solution:
   In a large dishpan, mix ½ gallon of water; 2 cups of dishwashing liquid (clear, lemon scented); 3 teaspoons of sugar (for viscosity); and 2 teaspoons of glycerine (optional).

3. Explain to the children that artists use light to "fool the eye." Tell the children that they can do it, too. Conduct a simple demonstration by placing a pen in a clear glass that has been half filled with water. Have the children stand back and look at the glass. What seems to have happened to the pen? *Refraction* is the key word here. Ask the children to think about how lenses refract light. Why is this helpful? (Refraction is the ability of the eye to bend light to focus an image on the retina.)

4. Ask the children if it is true that white light is made up of different colors. Write their responses on a piece of chart paper and then test their answers by using a prism. For further enrichment, have them compare their findings to the work of English physicist Isaac Newton. What did he find out in 1704 in his book *Opticks?* Look up this scientist on the Internet or in an encyclopedia to find the information you need.

Character Education Enrichment

1. Invite the children to write a letter to Elena's teacher seeking a solution to the problem. Ask them to use a scripture verse that fits the situation.

2. Give each child a copy of page 25 to use to create a list of the special qualities of each child in the class. Each child is to record the names of his or her classmates and then list one or more qualities that God gave each of these people to make him or her special. Keep the papers anonymous, but post them in the classroom.

3. One of the most talented artists in the Bible is the psalmist David. Invite the children to select a favorite psalm and analyze it from an artistic perspective. Give the children copies of page 26 to help them.

I Am Really an Artist

Character Education Enrichment continued

4. Guide the children in creating a "handprint" mural for the school that celebrates their individual differences. Use a large roll of white butcher or bulletin board paper for a background and then give each child the opportunity to dip his or her hand in tempera paint to make a handprint on the mural. When the prints are dried, each child should write his or her name and a statement of how God made him or her unique on the print or under it.

5. "D is for Differences" can become your slogan for a day of thinking and learning devoted to the identification and celebration of unique talents given to the children by God. Begin the day by cutting out a large letter "D" from tagboard or butcher paper (2 feet wide by 3 feet high). Then invite each child to use the dictionary and thesaurus to find an unusual and interesting "D" word that describes him or her. Here are some examples: Daring Michael; Direct Anna; Diminutive Meg; Dapper Enrico. The children then record their "D" phrases and any illustrations that they like on the large classroom "D."

6. Assign small groups of children a "Character Hunt" using vibrant, interesting Biblical characters and copies of page 27. Ask each group to use its research skills to complete the page.

7. Close this unit by inviting the children to pray for forgiveness if they have called another child an unkind name because of "differences," such as wearing glasses or not having fashionable clothes.

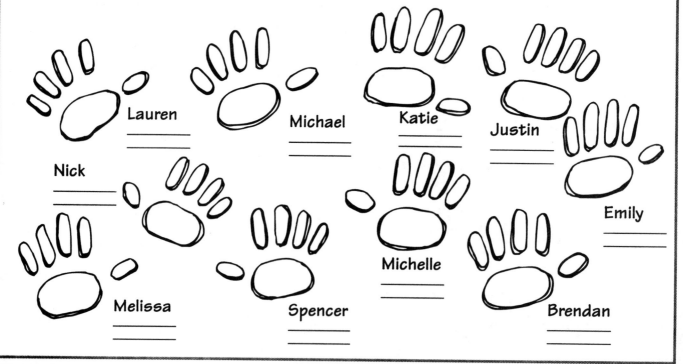

Interview With an Artist

Use this page to prepare your questions for your interview with an artist.

Name of the artist _____

1. What kind of art do you specialize in? _____
    _____

2. Can you tell me about the gifts that God gave you that helped you to become an artist? _____
    _____

3. Did you ever feel different from other children because of your abilities? _____
    _____

4. Do you feel that you use your art to give God glory? _____
    _____
    _____

5. What advice would you give someone who wants to be an artist?
    _____
    _____
    _____

Other questions: _____

_____

_____

_____

_____

_____

_____

_____

Name _____

License Plate Fun

Use the pattern below to create your own original nameplate.

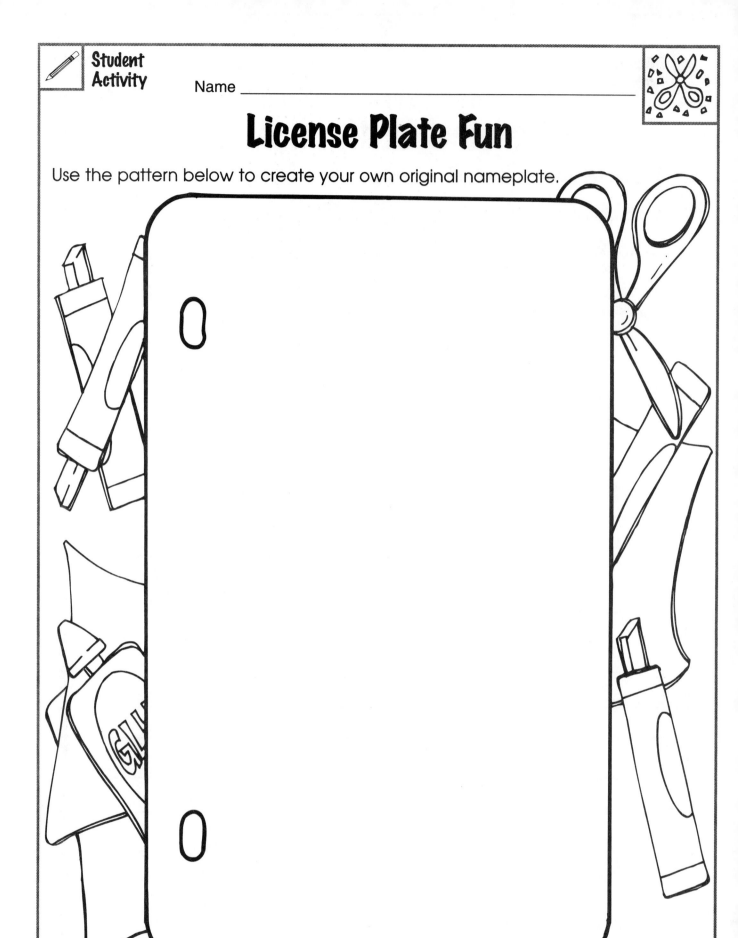

Secret Pals Are Special

Student Names	Special Abilities and Gifts

Favorite Psalm

Select your favorite psalm and answer the questions below using verses from the psalm.

My favorite psalm is _____

I chose this psalm because _____

_____

I like the way the psalmist described _____

_____

This psalm makes me feel _____

_____

_____

I think God gave David the gift of writing because _____

_____

_____

_____

_____

Illustrate an image from the psalm below.

Character Hunt

Team Members _____

Date _____ Teacher _____

Our Biblical Character _____

His or her story is found_____

Summary of the story _____

_____

_____

_____

_____

Three words that describe this person's talents or gifts are

_____, _____, _____.

This person used his or her talents to solve a problem or to serve God

by _____

_____

If this person had acted differently, the story might have turned out differently because . . .

_____

_____

_____

_____

_____

More Than Just a Wagon
A Story About Experiencing the Joy Found in Showing Kindness

by Dr. Linda Karges-Bone

Bible Verse to Learn: *Keep on loving each other as brothers. Do not forget to entertain strangers, for by so doing some people have entertained angels without knowing it.* (Hebrews 13:1–2)

"Turn here! Turn here!" eight-year-old Reid yelled as his dad pulled the old red pickup truck into a driveway. Reid had noticed the brightly-lettered sign on the way home from the recycling center that sunny Saturday morning. The sign read "Yard Sale."

"Now you know that in-line skates cost a lot," Reid's dad reminded him. "You've got five dollars of birthday money from Granny. Do you think you'll find in-line skates for five dollars?"

"You found that great fishing rod last Saturday, and Mom and Granny got an exercise machine at a yard sale."

"That's right. The 'Tummy Terrific Machine.' That lasted for about a week," laughed Reid's dad. Reid's mom was always trying out new ways to get thinner, especially since his new baby sister had arrived.

Thirty minutes later, Reid's face was glum. "I saw a sewing machine, a pile of plasticware pieces, old shoes, and magazines. But no in-line skates. Let's go, Dad."

"Wait a minute, Son. Let me take a look at this table saw, the one sitting in the red . . . hey, look at this!" exclaimed Reid's dad.

"Look at what?" asked Reid. He didn't feel too excited. There was no way that he could get new in-line skates. They just cost too much money, and his family didn't have a lot of money.

"Check out this wagon, Son. It's in good shape. The wheels move like new, and there's only a few scratches here and there. What about this for a present?"

"I don't know, Dad. What can you do with an old wagon? Nobody plays with wagons," replied Reid.

. . . Wagon continued

"I tell you, Son, I had a wagon when I was a boy, and it was great," said Reid's father. "My brother, your Uncle Andy, and I did some neat things with our wagon."

Reid perked up a little bit as his dad shared some interesting stories about himself, Uncle Andy, and the red wagon that they had played with. Maybe there was something about a wagon. He might as well try it. In-line skates seemed to be rolling out of his reach anyway.

Reid gave the lady his five-dollar bill, and she gave him back a rumpled green one-dollar bill. "Four dollars only, young man," said the smiling lady who was holding the yard sale. "Enjoy your wagon. It used to belong to my children, but they're off at college now. We're cleaning out our garage to make room for the ten-speed bicycles my husband and I are going to be riding."

Pulling the new purchase toward his dad's truck, Reid heard a friendly voice say, "Excuse me young man. Could you use that red wagon to help me get this box of records to my car?"

A small young lady wearing a black dancer's leotard and tights under a bright pink skirt pointed to a box of old records at her feet. "I teach jazz and tap at a studio downtown. These old albums have some wonderful music. But the box is quite heavy. Do you mind?" asked the lady.

Reid's dad lifted the box into the wagon, and Reid pulled his load down the block to where the young dancer's car was parked. "Thank you so much," she smiled, and before Reid or his dad could say anything, she tossed a dollar bill out the window to Reid and sped away.

"Thank you!" Reid called after the kind lady.

...Wagon continued

Later that day, Reid pulled his wagon out of the garage and down the sidewalk. He was going to show it to his best friend, Sam. On the way to Sam's house, he passed old Mrs. Jenkins.

"Hi Mrs J," called Reid.

"Is that a wagon?" Mrs. Jenkins called from her porch. "Come on up here, dear."

It turned out that Mrs. Jenkins needed some help moving bedding plants from the back of her minivan to the flower beds at the side of her house. She loaded 12 flats of purple and yellow blooms into Reid's wagon, and he pulled them around to the garden spot.

"That was a big help," said Mrs. Jenkins. "Here's a little something for your trouble." She handed Reid four quarters.

"You don't need to pay me," Reid told her. "I liked helping you."

"Well, I enjoyed it, too," agreed Mrs. Jenkins. "Let's just call it rent on your vehicle. Okay?"

When he finally got to Sam's, he found his best friend sitting on the porch with his younger sister, Amy, beside him.

"Mom is canning tomatoes with my aunts," began Sam. "We're not allowed inside right now. The kitchen is full of grumpy aunts and mom and boiling pots of tomatoes."

"That sounds bad," said Reid. So they took turns pulling Amy around in the wagon. She was three years old and kept saying, "Go again. Go again."

A while later, Sam's mom came outside. "Your mother wants you to come home now, Reid. She just called. I saw you fellows playing so nicely with Amy. That was a big help. Thank you both."

... Wagon continued

She carefully placed a warm jar of stewed tomatoes into the wagon, saying, "for your mom." Then she surprised Sam and Reid by handing each of them a dollar bill.

"You don't have to pay us," Reid said.

"But you can if you want to," finished Sam. He glared at Reid, who quickly put the money in his pocket, next to the quarters from Mrs. Jenkins and the money from the dancing lady. On the way home, Reid thought about the wagon. It was like a magnet, pulling money in. Was it okay to take the money for helping people? He wasn't sure.

During the next few weeks, Reid found a lot of uses for his wagon. He and Sam used it to collect aluminum cans from the neighbors. They took turns each week bringing the cans to the recycling center. So far, Reid had collected almost three dollars from his share of the recycling booty.

The wagon became a space shuttle, hurtling through the solar system toward Mars, when the boys draped a blue tablecloth over their heads.

One afternoon, the wagon became a boat, with fishing poles dangling plastic worms draped over the side. That was when Reid and Sam pulled it into a plastic wading pool filled part way up with water. "Are you catching anything?" Sam asked. Reid laughed.

As the autumn days grew shorter, Reid helped his dad rake leaves and burn them. Some of the leaves, however, they saved for compost, to nourish the ground for next summer's garden. Reid used his wagon to haul leaves to the compost pile.

Collecting pine cones to burn in the fireplace and for Reid's mom to use to decorate for the church bazaar gave the wagon another busy afternoon. Was there no end to the wonders of the wheeled box? Reid pondered this thought: "How had he ever gotten along without the wagon?"

 GP275702 Developing Character in Christian Kids

... Wagon continued

By Thanksgiving, Reid had collected over 20 dollars, between his weekly allowance for doing chores, his recycling money, and more surprising payments for jobs done with the wagon. In fact, his mom had given him two dollars of the money that she made selling pine cone angel ornaments at the Crafty Lady Shop downtown. After all, he had collected the pine cones and glued the lace wings on those angel ornaments.

"Are you going to buy some in-line skates with all your money?" asked Sam. They were busy pulling bricks from the curb to Mr. Washington's backyard. Their neighbor had a load of brown bricks delivered that morning that he was going to use to build an outside barbecue pit.

"I might," said Reid. "Especially since my mom said that the lady who owns the Crafty Lady is going to be selling her son's old pair at a yard sale next Saturday. Mom says they are really cool and look like new. The lady's son had a growth spurt, overnight or something, and outgrew them."

"Cool," said Sam.

But when Saturday came, a surprising thing happened to Reid. The in-line skates were for sale all right, but so was a fishing rod that his dad would have liked to have. Then Reid spied a set of blue glasses that exactly matched his mom's favorite dishes. But what really caught his eye was a big stuffed yellow teddy bear with brown eyes, just like his new baby sister's.

"Wow! I bet the baby would crawl all over that bear if it was under the Christmas tree," thought Reid. Before he knew what happened, the handy wagon was loaded with a fishing pole, a set of blue glasses, and a big yellow teddy bear.

"Ho, Ho, Ho! Merry Christmas!" Reid bellowed as he pulled the wagon into his own driveway. He felt really good, all warm inside. The red wagon had turned out to be more than just a toy. It was like a friend and an adventure on wheels.

More Than Just a Wagon

Language Arts

1. Use the outline of the wagon on page 36 to create a large wagon on a sheet of chart paper, or use the outline to create an overhead transparency. Then ask the children this question: *How many ways could you use a wagon?* Record the responses on the wagon outline. Use a red marker for visual enhancement.

2. "Wagon Loads of Kindness"—Use the wagon pattern on page 36 to create an outline of a wagon on red construction paper for each child. Send home the wagon with each child along with instructions for him or her to look for magazine pictures of scenes in which children are showing kindness to others. They are to cut and paste the scenes onto their wagon outlines and write a short paragraph on the back describing the kinds of activities that children might engage in to show kindness to others.

3. "W" Words—Use the hand pattern on page 36 to introduce the children to these critical questioning words: *Who? What? When? Where? Why?* The children can cut out their "W hands" and glue them to tongue depressors for easy manipulation. Discuss the story, "More Than Just a Wagon," in terms of each of the words. (Examples: **Who** is Reid? **What** are some ways that Reid used his wagon? **What** holiday did we hear about in the story? **Why** is it good to think of many ways to use our toys? **Where** did Reid take his wagon?) Children can raise their "hands" to respond.

Problem Solving

1. Bring a real wagon to the classroom for this problem-solving assignment. Each day, give teams of children the assignment of creating a way to use the wagon to make working and learning better or more efficient. Keep a list of each team's ideas. Make sure that the teams actually practice their ideas on that day. For example, the wagon might be used to bring the daily milk containers down to the kindergarten classroom.

2. Tell the children that a wagon is a wonderful toy and a wonderful tool. Then challenge them to think of ways to improve the wagon. How can a wagon literally become more than a wagon? Let the children record their ideas on copies of the wagon pattern (page 36).

3. Give the children math practice using word problems involving the wagon you brought in. Give teams of children pencils, paper, and the math word problems on the top of page 34 to make practicing math skills more stimulating. As the children's skills improve, bring in a timer to give the teams competition.

More Than Just a Wagon

Problem Solving continued

Math Problems

- The wagon contains 6 pounds of sugar. How many ounces of sugar are in the wagon? (Answer: 96 oz.)

- The wagon is carrying 10 bags of paper plates. Each bag holds 100 paper plates. Will there be enough plates to serve the 500 people that are expected at the church picnic? (Answer: Yes, because there will be 1,000 paper plates.)

- The wagon can hold up to 200 pounds of cargo. If Emily, who weighs 62 pounds, Carlos, who weighs 68 pounds, and Frances, who weighs 50 pounds, all ride in the wagon at the same time, will the wagon be able to hold the load? (Answer: Yes, because the combined weight of the children is 180 lb.)

- How long will it take Fred to pull the wagon to the recycling bin if the bin is one mile from the school and he travels at a rate of 3 miles per hour? (Answer: 20 minutes)

4. Let the children problem solve with blocks and the wagon to give children a lesson in force, weight, and distribution of energy! To do this, assign each team of four children a stack of 500 wooden blocks of different sizes and shapes. (Each team must have the same blocks and the same time allotment of 10 minutes.) Then give each team a chance to stack up as many blocks as it can and pull its pyramid around a pre-set perimeter. The goal is for the blocks to stay standing while the wagon is in motion. Ask the children to observe how the distribution of the blocks impacts balance. How did the teams work together to solve the problem? Which team's work produced the best results and why?

Creative Arts

1. Provide streamers, wrapping paper scraps, felt, ribbon, and other materials the children can use to decorate the real wagon for the holiday season. How might the wagon look in an African celebration? a South American celebration? an Asian celebration?

2. Guide the children in baking and decorating cookies and place them in tins or whipped topping bowls that are easily stacked. Stack them in your real wagon and have the children deliver them to a rest home or elder care facility, the school custodian, the school librarian, or a sick child in the area. Talk about how good it feels to help.

More Than Just a Wagon

Character Education Enrichment

1. When the children do the baking activity described in Creative Arts Activity 2, extend it by inviting each child to select a favorite Bible verse about kindness and giving and using them to create labels for the containers. Apply the labels to the containers for decoration and inspiration.

2. Lead the children in a discussion of the Bible verse to remember from page 28, Hebrews 13:1–2. Ask them to think of situations in which they or a family member showed kindness that turned out in an unexpected way. Was someone surprised, moved, angered by the act of kindness? What might cause someone to behave in that way?

3. Let each child prepare a "Kindness Coupon" booklet for his or her family using three copies of page 37 per child. To make the booklet, have the children cut apart the coupons and staple them together on the left-hand side. Make sure children put all three like coupons behind each other. On each coupon/page of the booklet, the children complete the sentences to determine acts of service or kindness (not regular chores) that they will offer up for their families.

4. Set up a classroom "Kindness Counts" jar. Simply place a large, empty jar on your desk and invite children to write their private acts of kindness on slips of paper, which are then placed in the jar. These slips of paper should be anonymous. On Friday afternoon, read a few slips aloud and offer up prayers of thanksgiving for the opportunity to serve others. The children should be taught that these acts should remain anonymous. Showing kindness should often be private, and one should not expect thanks.

5. Ask the children to think about situations in which Jesus showed kindness. What was kind? Was it his actions? his tone of voice? his concern? Give the children copies of page 38 to use to respond to these questions.

More Than Just a Wagon
Patterns

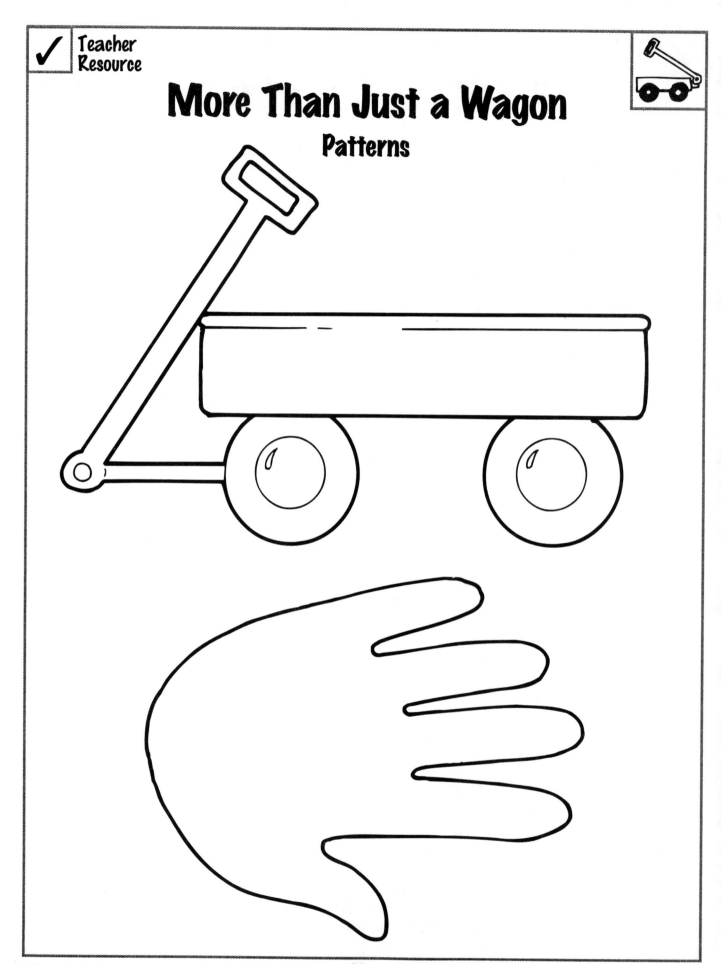

GP275702 Developing Character in Christian Kids

Kindness Coupon Booklet

My Kindness Coupon Booklet

_____
(name)

I will offer my time to help _____

by _____

_____.

I will surprise _____ with this act

of kindness: _____

_____.

I will show kindness to _____ to

celebrate _____.
(birthday, anniversary, Mother's Day, etc.)

Name _____

Jesus Teaches About Kindness

For each letter of the word KINDNESS, write about a situation in which Jesus showed kindness or a Bible verse in which he taught about showing kindness. You may work with a partner.

K _____

_____

I _____

_____

N _____

_____

D _____

_____

N _____

_____

E _____

_____

S _____

_____

S _____

_____

Write your favorite Bible verse about kindness.

_____

_____

Yard of the Month

A Story About Learning to Become
Good Citizens and Servants

by Dr. Linda Karges-Bone

Bible Verse to Learn: . . . *"If anyone wants to be first, he must be the very last, and the servant of all."* (Mark 9:35)

LaTasha quickly checked the answers on her math paper. It was fun to check subtraction problems by adding the answer with the amount being subtracted. LaTasha felt good because only one of her problems needed to be corrected. Carefully counting in her head, LaTasha finished the problem. She walked to the front of the classroom and placed her work in the blue basket that held daily math papers for grading. Mrs. Washington, her fourth-grade teacher, turned from the board where she had been writing new spelling words and smiled at LaTasha.

"I like the way everyone is completing the math lesson this morning," said Mrs. Washington. "That gives us just enough time to read a new fable before lunch."

LaTasha glided back to her desk. "I can hardly wait for the latest fable," she thought. "Fables must be the most interesting and exciting kind of story in the world," mused LaTasha.

"Come and sit on the story rug," invited Mrs. Washington, using her mysterious story-reading voice.

The children settled on a brightly-colored rag rug that Mrs. Washington had brought back from her summer trip to the Holy Land. Leaning forward on the wicker rocking chair, the teacher read in a clear voice:

Once there was an old woman who was very poor. She lived in a small, dirty cottage with broken windows and tattered curtains. She had a little food from her garden and a goat that she kept for milking. The old woman felt very sorry for herself. Every day, she would think, "Surely no person in the world could be as poor and worthless as I am."

Yard of the Month continued

Then one morning, the old woman hobbled out to her garden to weed the turnips and potatoes. She did not feel the warmth of the sun nor see the colors in a delicate butterfly nor hear the musical songs of the birds because she was so bitter and felt so sorry for herself. As she turned the soil over with her trowel, the old woman felt something hard and smooth hit her tool. She pulled a slender golden vase from the dirt. Although it was tarnished and crusted with dirt, the old woman could see that it had once been quite beautiful.

"Perhaps a merchant dropped this from his pack many years ago," thought the old woman. "Let me see if it can be restored and then maybe I can sell it to buy some cloth and tea."

So the old woman wrapped the vase in her apron and carried it into the cottage. She washed away the dirt with soapy water and patted the vase dry. "Hmmm, it certainly looks better. Let me do a bit more," she mused.

Then the old woman took a few drops of oil and polished the vase gently with a soft rag. Soon the vase shone golden and glorious. The old woman felt pleased with her efforts. "Perhaps I will keep the vase for a day or two before selling it," she decided.

When the old woman placed the lovely vase on her kitchen table, she said, "This table looks so dirty now that a treasure is sitting upon it." Taking her brush, she scrubbed her table clean. Then the old woman went to her cedar chest and pulled a piece of lace out that she had been given as a bride but had never used. The lace made a fine table cover. Placing it on the clean table, the old woman stood back and admired. "The table looks better," she decided, "but now the floor needs cleaning."

Yard of the Month continued

The old woman took a broom and mop and cleaned the floor of her small cottage. The worn brown boards shone soft and smooth. "Hmmm, the floor looks much better, but now the windows need washing so that the light can shine in."

The old woman took down her dusty curtains and washed the windows with vinegar and water. Then the bright sunlight poured into her clean, little home. The old woman was smiling now. Her step was light as she walked into the neighboring field to pick some wildflowers to fill the golden vase.

As the afternoon closed, the old woman brewed a cup of lemon tea and sat at the table. She felt refreshed and pleased with herself. "Perhaps life is not so bad," she thought.

Mrs. Washington closed the book and asked the children, "What lesson was God teaching the old woman?"

Anthony raised his hand, "She learned that God likes us to be clean."

Joy Lynn raised her hand, "The old woman learned that God wants us to work hard."

Then LaTasha spoke up, "I think God wants us to serve him and to make the best of whatever circumstance we are in. We can make the world better no matter how poor we are."

Mrs. Washington nodded her head. "You all have something truthful and important to say, but LaTasha, you are definitely on to something big!"

As LaTasha rode home in the school bus that afternoon, her head was full of ideas. Her neighborhood looked rundown and dusty, much like the old woman's cottage. But LaTasha had an idea. Maybe she could make people want to change like the old woman in the fable had done.

Yard of the Month continued

At supper that evening, LaTasha told her family about the fable and about her plan. Her father, who was a carpenter, said that he would help LaTasha with her plan. "I think you are on to something big!" He grinned at his little daughter.

LaTasha and her father worked in the garage until ten o'clock that night. They sawed and trimmed and sanded and painted. Pleased with their work, LaTasha and her father and mother munched some peanut butter crackers. The next day was Saturday. LaTasha would unveil her plan to the neighborhood.

Saturday morning, LaTasha's mother invited the seven families that lived on West Avenue to a meeting. The families began to arrive around three o'clock. LaTasha's mother served iced tea and sugar cookies, making everyone comfortable. Then LaTasha's father stood up and spoke.

"Our neighborhood could be much nicer if we just spent a little time trimming the bushes, cleaning up litter, and even planting some flowers. Little things can make a big improvement, and we can help one another to make these changes. My daughter LaTasha thought of the idea of having a 'Yard of the Month' award to be given to the family that has kept their yard the nicest each month."

LaTasha held up the sign. It was a wonderful sign, painted white with dark green lettering that read YARD OF THE MONTH. A trail of small pink and purple posies curved around the border of the sign. The neighbors nodded their approval.

Over the next few weeks, the neighbors on West Avenue spent a lot more time working in their yards. Like the old woman in the fable, it seemed that every little change made folks want to do a bit more. LaTasha took every opportunity to encourage and to serve.

GP275702 Developing Character in Christian Kids

Yard of the Month continued

When the Gomez family trimmed their bushes and planted a border of flowers down the walkway, LaTasha helped put the bedding plants in.

Mrs. Anderson and her daughters raked leaves and pine straw and set out pots of autumn mums, and LaTasha pitched in.

LaTasha's aunt and uncle, who lived next door, started collecting newspapers and bottles for recycling, and she brought a bin around to each home on West Avenue. Things were looking fine.

When the month was over, almost every family had tried hard to make the street look neat and attractive. But one yard remained cluttered and messy. LaTasha felt bad about this and talked with her parents about the Millers' home. "Why don't they try like everyone else?" she asked.

"Sometimes folks have a hard heart," offered her mother.

"Sometimes people get depressed," added her father.

"What are we supposed to do?" asked LaTasha.

"Let's pray for the Millers," her parents said, and they did.

On the next Saturday, the neighbors met to vote on which family should have the YARD OF THE MONTH sign posted in their grass for the next month. Each family had one vote and LaTasha counted them all.

"The Jordan family wins the sign for this month!" announced LaTasha. She felt good. The Jordan family had painted their porch and hauled away some old trash and toys from their yard. In fact, the whole street looked better.

"People can change," she thought. And it felt good to be a part of that.

GP275702 Developing Character in Christian Kids

Yard of the Month

Language Arts

1. Write the terms *fable* and *parable* on the board. Brainstorm with the children a list of similarities and differences between the two terms. Then tell the children to use dictionaries to write precise definitions of each in their vocabulary notebooks.

2. Give the children copies of page 47 to use to write a newspaper advertisement for a "servant." Invite the children to think about what a servant does and can do.

3. Review the format for a business letter (Heading, Inside Address, Salutation, Body, Complimentary Close, Signature) and then guide the children in writing a whole class "Letter to the Editor" of your local paper, commenting on an important social issue about which the children feel strongly.

4. The heroine of the story, LaTasha, solved a problem because of her persistence and desire to make the world a better place. Each child in your class has qualities that make him or her capable of doing great things, and creating a "Poem About Me" can be a useful task in language arts and in recognizing strengths. Give each child a copy of page 48 he or she can use to create his or her poem. (You might also want to put a copy of it on an overhead projector.)

5. Using home improvement and lawn and garden magazines, help the children locate adjectives and adverbs and notice how they are used in descriptive writing or in directions for projects. Begin by putting a page of text on an overhead transparency. Show the children examples of adjectives and adverbs in the narrative writing. You may want to use one color of marking pen to identify adjectives and another color for adverbs. Once the children seem to understand the concept, reproduce pages of text for teams of children to use in finding adjectives and adverbs. Below are suggestions of activities the children can do to further enhance their understanding of adjectives and adverbs.

   • Circle all the adjectives in blue and all the adverbs in red.

   • Make a list of adjectives and a list of adverbs.

   • Find adjectives and adverbs and then use marking tape to cover these words. Write over the tape with new and more interesting choices of describing words.

   • Look in a Bible. Make a list of ten adverbs and ten adjectives you find.

   • Write a favorite Bible story in your own words. Use at least five adjectives and five adverbs in it.

   • Write a prayer to God. Use as many adjectives and adverbs in it as you can.

Yard of the Month

Creative Arts

1. Give each group of 3–4 children a piece of posterboard, paint, stencils, glitter, markers, and other art materials to use to create original YARD OF THE MONTH signs for their neighborhoods.

2. Provide each group of 3–4 students with a piece of posterboard, magazines, scissors, and glue. Guide the children in selecting pictures from magazines that show "citizens" and "servants" and have them create collages with that same title.

3. Bring in old home improvement and lawn and garden magazines. Invite the children to look through them and cut out pictures of homes and yards that look inviting or appealing. Each child or pair of children can glue their favorite home and/or yard to a piece of paper and finish the sentences below, which you write on the board.

   - *This house looks friendly to me because of the way it . . .*

   - *The colors on this house are _____, _____, and _____, and I like them because . . .*

   - *I would like to live in this house or play in this yard because . . .*

4. Collect paint samples from discount or paint stores. Place them in margarine or whipped topping tubs organized by color. (This is a great job for the children.) Then give each child a copy of page 49, which asks him or her to sketch a favorite room in his or her house and to "re-do" it with color. For example, a child might use a light blue color strip on his or her reading chair and a cool green for the walls.

5. Give each child colored markers and drawing paper and invite the children to draw the "Perfect Backyard." Would there be scented flowers? a cool blue pool? a tree to climb? Play restful, classical music in the background as the children imagine and create their perfect backyard retreats.

Character Building Enrichment

1. Lead a group discussion of the Bible verse for this story (Mark 9:35). Ask the children to discuss what they think the verse means for Christians and then create a list of public figures who model this kind of living in their lives and work.

2. In a group discussion, ask the children to contribute examples of how family members can serve one another. Write the children's responses on a piece of chart paper and display it as a daily reminder.

Yard of the Month

Character Building Enrichment continued

3. Write the words CITIZEN and SERVANT on the board. Ask the children to think of ways that citizens and servants can have common goals. The children can use copies of page 50 to help them elaborate on this concept.

4. Invite a government leader, such as a member of the school board or city council, to come for a visit. Look around for someone who is "real," and not a particularly high-ranking official, so that the children will be able to identify with him or her. Your goal is to bring in someone who is not paid for his or her work and who serves part-time in his or her position while also attending to a full-time job. The children ask these and other questions:

   • *How do you do your full-time job and still find time to serve?*

   • *When you were a child, did you ever think that you would serve as a government leader?*

   • *Why do you think it is important for citizens to serve on boards?*

   • *What accomplishments do you want people to remember during your service?*

   • *Do your values ever clash with your duties?*

5. "Think Through the Problem" is an exercise in problem solving and character building. Write each of the scenarios below on a strip of paper. Then put them in a covered tin or box. Seat the children in a circle and place a small foam ball in the center of the circle. Invite one child to choose one of the "think through" scenarios and another to "start the ball rolling." The children will respond to the challenge with Biblically sound solutions, and they will take their turns by having the ball thrown to them by a classmate. Each child may have the ball one time per scenario and can only respond with a single sentence. The scenario is "solved" when you stop the session or when a child holding the ball says, "We solved it."

Scenarios

• The "Yard of the Month" sign is stolen or defaced with paint.

• The neighbors argue over who should receive the award.

• One neighbor always seems to do the very best on his or her yard and wins all the time.

• LaTasha loses interest in the project.

• A new family moves in, and they do not want to participate in Yard of the Month.

Name _____

Wanted: Willing Servant

Study the classified advertisements in the newspaper. Then write a one-page advertisement for a servant. The salary, jobs, and skills needed are up to you to decide.

_____

_____

_____

_____

_____

_____

_____

_____

_____

_____

_____

_____

_____

_____

_____

_____

_____

_____

_____

_____

Name _____

A Poem About Me

Complete the poem below with words that describe the unique qualities given to you by God.

_____
first name

I am very good at _____

_____

Sometimes I worry about _____

_____

When life gets hard, I try to _____

_____

People can always count on me to _____

_____

Three words that describe me are

_____

_____

_____

_____
last name

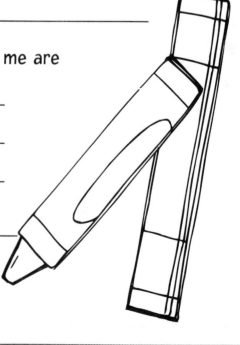

My Favorite Room

Use the paint samples or colored pencils to create a room that makes you feel content and relaxed. What colors will you use for the walls, floor, rugs, furniture, and fixtures? Sketch your design below and then glue a paint sample on or under the objects in your sketch to show your color choices.

My Favorite Room

by _____

Name _____

Common Characteristics

Under each column, write characteristics of each kind of person, *citizen* and *servant*. Circle the characteristics that both have in common with a red pen or pencil.

Citizen	Servant
_____	_____
_____	_____
_____	_____
_____	_____
_____	_____
_____	_____
_____	_____
_____	_____
_____	_____
_____	_____
_____	_____
_____	_____
_____	_____
_____	_____
_____	_____
_____	_____
_____	_____
_____	_____

Rescue on the Cedar Island Ferry

A Story About Developing a Sense of Personal Responsibility and Integrity

by Dr. Linda Karges-Bone

Bible Verse To Learn: *Let us not become weary in doing good, for at the proper time we will reap a harvest if we do not give up.* (Galatians 6:9)

The breeze off Pamlico Sound felt more like a Canadian chill than a North Carolina autumn, but twelve-year-old twins, Natalie and Nathanial, decided to stay outside and hang on to the gleaming rails of the Cedar Island ferry as it cut smoothly through the green water.

"I can't believe we have to spend Thanksgiving with Grandma and Grandpa. It is so boring there," began Nathanial.

"Out on that island, with no television even. Gee, you would think with satellite dishes and cable and everything, Grandpa would get with the program," added his sister.

"Yeah, but Grandpa was born in 1927 on Ocracoke Island, and that's how he likes things, old-fashioned," returned Nat.

"And boring," finished Natalie.

The twins gazed out at the sound. At least this part of the trip was interesting, a two hour and fifteen minute journey on the ferry, across the emerald green waters of Pamlico Sound, a large lagoon on the east coast of the United States. It was the Wednesday before Thanksgiving, and the twins were on their way to spend it with their grandparents, on Ocracoke Island, part of the North Carolina Banks.

"It looks like we're out in the middle of the ocean," breathed Natalie. "Even though I know the coast is out there somewhere, it is weird to have so much water all around."

Rescue ... continued

"Actually, it is just on three sides. That's what a lagoon is, water on three sides," instructed Nathanial, winner of the sixth-grade geography competition.

"Thank you, Mr. Geo-Wizard," laughed his sister. Her interest was in science, and she pointed out the gulls, fish, and even a distant porpoise to her brother as they traveled along in the cold November afternoon. After catching the 1:00 p.m. ferry, they expected to arrive at Ocracoke Island after 3:00 p.m. The ferry or a private boat or small plane were the only means of connecting Ocracoke Island to the outside world.

"I can't believe Mom and Dad want to take a romantic second honeymoon over our Thanksgiving break," Natalie said. "They're too old for that kind of thing anyway."

"And leave us out in the wilderness with Grandpa and Grandma and those strange little horses," added Nat.

"Well, I like the little horses," Natalie returned. She was thinking about becoming a veterinarian, and the herd of small horses penned on Ocracoke Island fascinated her. The story went that the herd of horses on Ocracoke Island were descendants of special Spanish horses that had swum ashore hundreds of years earlier when the ship that they were traveling on had been shipwrecked in a vicious Outer Banks storm.

"Imagine if we had been alive that night when the ship wrecked and the horses swam ashore," dreamed Natalie, out loud.

"Oh no. Here we go again," groaned her brother. "Saint Natalie, rescuer of all stranded animals."

"I guess it is in my blood, with Grandpa taking care of the horses on Ocracoke, and Mom being a veterinarian, too. It's my destiny," replied Natalie.

GP275702 Developing Character in Christian Kids

Rescue . . . continued

"Well, my destiny is to go inside and get some hot chocolate out of that vending machine. I'm about to freeze," said Nathanial, rubbing his gloved hands together in anticipation.

"Wait a minute," interrupted Natalie. "What is that in the water?"

"Hey, it's a dog, a Labrador retriever," identified Nat. "But what's a black lab doing in the middle of Pamlico Sound?"

"I'll bet he fell off a boat or one of the earlier ferries," said Natalie. "We've got to rescue that dog. You go and get help. I'll stay here and call to the dog to keep its spirits up."

Nat ran into the passenger lounge where he had seen a crew member of the Cedar Island ferry. He returned with two adults, a sturdy looking woman named Amanda, and a thin, young man named Jack. Amanda wore the official khaki uniform of the North Carolina Ferry Service, but Jack wore jeans and a sweatshirt that read "College of Charleston." Later, they would learn that he was doing an internship for the marine biology program.

"The pilot is slowing the ferry down so that we can put a rescue craft in the water," said Amanda. "Let's get some blankets ready to rub that dog down."

The children watched and waited with their blankets as Amanda and Jack lowered the lifeboat and then churned toward the floundering black dog. It took about 15 minutes for the rescue to be completed. In the meantime, a small crowd of passengers had gathered.

"What will happen to the poor dog?" asked one man.

"We'll take her to Ocracoke with us," said Nat and Natalie in unison. That was one interesting aspect of being a twin, thinking the same thing at the same time.

The twins welcomed the shivering black lab and wrapped it in thick gray blankets. Jack helped carry her to the passenger lounge where it was warm and dry.

"No reports on the radio," said the pilot of the ferry when he came down to check on the rescue crew and the dog. "I guess you kids can take her home for now. We'll get your telephone number on Ocracoke in case anybody gets in touch with us."

Rescue . . . continued

Fortunately, the twin's grandparents loved animals, too, and saw nothing unusual about bringing a four-legged guest home for Thanksgiving dinner. Grandpa's king-sized pickup truck had a cab big enough for the twins and their new friend.

"Let's see if she'll take some warm milk and scrambled eggs," said Grandma when they got home. By now, the black lab had stopped shivering and weakly licked at the children's hands.

"I called the vet, but she's gone away for Thanksgiving, too," said Grandpa when he returned to the warm kitchen of the farmhouse. "I think we're on our own for a few days."

"I got your veterinary book from the den," began Natalie, "and we're doing all the right things for exposure."

"Smart girl," said Grandma. "You'll be a veterinarian some day. You've got the instincts."

Nat and Natalie took turns keeping watch on their new pet, which Nat had named "Pam" because she had emerged from the waters of Pamlico Sound. "It is geographically correct," he pronounced.

Thursday morning was Thanksgiving. Pam had cried and whimpered a few times during the night, but each time, Nat and Natalie woke from their sleeping bags and comforted her. The trio had spent the night in front of the woodstove in the den, Pam on a thick braided rug, and the twins in their camping gear.

By two o'clock, the smell of roasting turkey filled the cozy farmhouse on Ocracoke. Friends gathered from around the island, including Jack from the ferry who couldn't afford to travel back to Charleston, South Carolina, to spend Thanksgiving with his family.

Grandma's Thanksgiving dinner was bountiful and delicious: roasted turkey, as well as a rosy Virginia ham, sweet potato casserole, rice and gravy, cranberry sauce, corn bread stuffing, and pickles that she had put up late in the summer. After dinner, they sat in the den and talked and laughed, and once again, told the story of the Cedar Island ferry rescue, this time to their guests. By evening, Pam had perked up considerably and was nibbling at a turkey leg.

Rescue ... continued

The twins eagerly told their version of the story, assisted by Jack. Then they listened as Grandpa recounted stories of other rescues off Ocracoke Island, fierce hurricanes in the fall, nor'easters in the winter, and sudden summer lightning storms.

Near ten o'clock, after consuming more turkey and then some of the Southern desserts of pecan pie, sweet potato pie, and something rich and gooey that one of the aunts called a "Hummingbird Cake," the twins nodded off.

The next day, Pam woke them by licking their faces. She was like a new dog, vigorous and bouncing. They all joined Grandpa on his twice daily trek to the horse pens to feed the Ocracoke ponies. Pam barked and chased and ran with the twins. They helped Grandpa with his work. Then they took out bicycles from the shed and cycled around the island. On Ocracoke, bicycles were the favorite means of transportation. Grandma had packed them a picnic lunch of cold turkey sandwiches, tangerines, and cookies. Nat and Natalie shared the lunch with Pam after stopping near a quiet dune on the beach.

"I can't believe we have to go back on Saturday," sighed Natalie.

"At least Pam will be here when we come back at Christmas," said Nat. "I hope it goes fast. I can't wait to get back to the island."

"Can you believe we thought it would be boring?" asked Natalie.

"No way. This is the best Thanksgiving we've ever had. I mean, look at all we have to be thankful for—our new dog, our new friend Jack, and . . . "

"And Grandma and Grandpa, too," the twins finished in unison.

The November sunshine was warm and direct for a few hours, and the twins cycled back to the farmhouse. Ocracoke Island seemed like a wonderful place to be, television or not, because of their Thanksgiving rescue on the Cedar Island ferry, and the lessons they learned about friends and family and responsibility.

Rescue on the Cedar Island Ferry

Language Arts

1. Guide the children in completing activity page 59. On it, they list ACTIVE or PASSIVE ways of being responsible. Lead the children in a discussion of how Christians are accountable to do good, not just to be good. This activity is helpful in teaching verbs and voice in language arts.

2. Guide the children in writing a letter to a Christian friend who may be growing weary in a tough situation. Review the parts of a friendly letter: Heading, Greeting, Body, Closing, and Signature.

3. Have the children investigate the words RESPONSIBILITY and INTEGRITY using the dictionary. Give them copies of activity page 60 to help them. Children can also search in the Bible for the words INTEGRITY and RESPONSIBILITY to find examples of how God uses them. Then they can read a few examples aloud together.

4. Let the children practice public speaking skills by asking them each to write and present a one-minute commercial entitled "Responsible Kid for Hire." Each child will be timed to make sure that his or her commercial is indeed one minute long and meets the following criteria:

   • Length (1 minute) _____

   • Speaks clearly and loud enough to be understood _____

   • Uses correct grammar and syntax _____

   • Explains why he or she has qualities that make him or her a responsible person _____

   • Uses interesting examples of why he or she would be a good choice _____

5. Invite the children to write a fresh ending for the story "Rescue on the Cedar Island Ferry." The children may work in teams of 2–3 to complete this writing task. When the finished works are ready, read them aloud to the entire class and ask each child to complete the following evaluation form:

   • Did the ending "fit in" with the rest of the story?

   • Did the new ending take a positive or a negative view of the characters?

   • What lessons could you learn from the new ending of the story?

   • How did the writers use dialogue to let you know how the story was going to end?

   • Did the new ending surprise you?

   • Was the new ending realistic or too fantastic?

Rescue on the Cedar Island Ferry

Creative Arts

1. Give children art paper, glitter, markers, glue, and crayons to create "Right on for Responsibility" cards to share with friends. These cards can be given to Christian friends who "do the right thing" even when it seems hard or when one is weary or worried. This activity helps children to become encouragers.

2. Guide the children in making Responsibility Paper Chains. Cut art paper into strips that children then decorate with designs and an imprint of their personal responsibilities. For example, a child might draw flowers on a strip that says "water plants for Mom." Use glue to make the strips into linked chains that can be hung from the classroom ceiling.

3. Cedar Island is a vacation spot, and many beautiful spots inspire stories and artwork. Collect some travel brochures from a local agent and set them up in a "Great Get-Away" center. Place the brochures, a cassette player, and blank cassette tapes in the center. During free time, invite children to select a brochure and record a "Great Get-Away" message using copies of page 61.

4. Using the same travel brochures described above as examples, have the children fold sheets of drawing paper into three-section "fold-outs." Give the children markers, stickers, stamps, and other art materials they can use to create brochures for Cedar Island.

Character Education Enrichment

1. Ask the children to think about this question: *Why is it hard to maintain integrity?* Brainstorm situations in which doing the right thing consistently can be difficult. Together, create a list of ways that Christian kids can maintain their integrity in spite of pressures. Then give the children copies of page 62 to complete.

2. Give the children copies of page 63 they can use to keep an "Eye on Integrity." Have the children respond to each situation. Then discuss the situations as a class.

3. A big part of character building is learning to "do the right thing," even when circumstances are difficult. Ask the children to make a list of "tough circumstances" that the twins or their friends found themselves in. Then discuss how their responses to those situations were character-rich or character-poor. Use copies of page 58 to help you. It makes a nice overhead transparency.

Certain Circumstances

"Tough" circumstances from the story

-
-
-
-
-

Responses of the characters

CHARACTER-RICH RESPONSES	CHARACTER-POOR RESPONSES
•	•
•	•
•	•
•	•
•	•

Are You Active or Passive?

Under each heading, list situations in which you find yourself actively involved in showing responsibility or integrity or situations in which you choose to be passive.

Active Christian	**Passive Christian**
_____	_____
_____	_____
_____	_____
_____	_____
_____	_____
_____	_____
_____	_____
_____	_____
_____	_____
_____	_____
_____	_____
_____	_____
_____	_____
_____	_____
_____	_____
_____	_____
_____	_____
_____	_____
_____	_____

Name _____

Word Search

Use a dictionary to research the root words, word origins, and meanings of the words *responsibility* and *integrity*. Then use each word in a sentence.

Word: **Responsibility**

Root Word _____ Origin _____

Definition _____

_____

_____

Sentence _____

_____

_____

Word: **Integrity**

Root Word _____ Origin _____

Definition _____

_____

_____

Sentence _____

_____

_____

The Great Get-Away

After looking at your travel brochure, write some notes about your "Great Get-Away." Then record a message about why this particular spot appeals to you. You can use your own words and the brochures for inspiration and facts. Just use this page to make notes for your audiotape.

My destination is _____.

I need to get away because _____
_____.

The brochure was interesting because I like to _____
_____.

Some of the sights I want to see on my get-away are
_____.

On my "Great Get-Away," I can't wait to _____
_____.

If I could take only three people with me on my get-away, they would be _____.

When I come back from my get-away, I will tell you all about _____.

I think God made this place special because _____
_____.

Name _____

Brainstorm on Integrity

A brainstorm is an actual "flurry" of activity in the brain. Use this outline of a human brain to record your ideas about maintaining integrity in spite of a tough situation. For example, you might write, "Remove yourself from the temptation" or "Pray for guidance" on your brain.

Eye on Integrity

Read each situation. Write a 2–3 sentence response and an appropriate Bible verse that supports your response.

Situation One: You have been collecting money for a school fundraiser and find out that a family friend has overpaid you by $5. That is exactly the amount that you need to buy your mom a nice birthday gift. What will you do?

Eye on Integrity: _____

_____

_____

Situation Two: One of your chores is feeding the dog. You forgot to give her fresh water yesterday, and your dad thinks that the dog simply knocked over her dish again. Wow! You got out of trouble this time. Right?

Eye on Integrity: _____

_____

_____

Situation Three: You really like the new girl in your class. She is so much fun to be around. But when you were walking to school the other day, she started talking badly about another friend, using bad words, and gossiping. You don't want to let this girl think that you aren't cool, so what will you do?

Eye on Integrity: _____

_____

_____

Situation Four: The science chapter test is really hard this time, and you haven't had a chance to study much with soccer practice going on. While you are taking the test, the genius-kid in front of you lets her paper show. It would be so easy to look and so nice to have that "A." Now what?

Eye on Integrity: _____

_____

_____

Emma Jane's Discovery
A Story About Developing a Commitment to Compassion

by Dr. Linda Karges-Bone

Bible Verse To Learn: *Jesus called his disciples to him and said: "I have compassion for these people; they have already been with me three days and have nothing to eat. I do not want to send them away hungry, or they may collapse on the way."* (Matthew 15:32)

Part One: Chicago, Illinois, 1889

The old lady's thin white fingers clasped the blue porcelain teacup as Jane Addams poured a fragrant brew. "I am so happy to have you here at Hull House," said the gentle Miss Addams, speaking in the woman's native Polish language.

"It is good to be with friends and to share delicious cookies similar to the kind we once had in the old country," smiled the elderly guest.

Jane Addams passed the silver platter, carefully arranged with tempting cookies and pastries. The ten Polish ladies, dressed in their colorful native costumes, had come to Hull House to share their beautiful crochet work, some hot tea, and warm conversation. Often, they had felt lonely and abandoned since leaving Europe to come as immigrants to America.

Although the younger folks seemed to learn the language with ease and the strange foreign customs as well, the older women longed for familiar surroundings and voices and for someone to appreciate their spinning, weaving, crochet work, and embroidery. At Hull House, they met someone who cared about them, their families, and their problems. They met Miss Jane Addams.

In 1889, Jane Addams, together with her friend Ellen Starr, moved into the home of Charles J. Hull in Chicago and used it for her dream of developing a settlement house among the poor and disheartened immigrants. She called the place Hull House. Here she set up many types of programs, from day nurseries to college courses, that people of every nation and race could take advantage of.

Emma Jane . . . continued

Working among the poor immigrants, Miss Addams helped people not only to become comfortable in America but also to remember and respect their own heritages. It was exciting, compassionate work, and Jane Addams loved it as much as people grew to love her.

Part Two: Charleston, South Carolina, 1999

Emma Jane Sullivan closed the worn, brown library book and leaned back in the porch swing. It was the third time she had read the biography of Jane Addams, and still the story left her feeling sort of funny inside, sort of restless and thoughtful.

"Jane Addams lived at Hull House exactly 110 years ago," mused Emma Jane. "She was helping people who had no homes, no friends, not much food. People really needed someone to care about them, and she was there. I wish there was a way for me to truly help people, not just give an offering at church or collect canned foods for the school food drive. I want to do something. I want to be like Jane Addams."

Emma Jane pulled her knees up to her chest and rocked back and forth in the swing. She was small for being almost 12 years old, and she was quiet by nature. Emma Jane was a thinker, but now she wanted to be a doer.

The screen door to the kitchen clunked shut, and Emma Jane heard her mother's pleasant voice, "Want to ride down to the church with me Emma J. and drop off this box of dinner rolls?"

"Sure, Mama," Emma Jane agreed. She hopped off the porch swing and opened her brown eyes wide in surprise. "There must be 50 boxes of dinner rolls in that big box! Who's going to eat all these rolls?" she asked.

"These rolls are for *Meals on Wheels*," answered her mother.

"What's *Meals on Wheels*?" asked Emma Jane, curiously.

Emma Jane . . . continued

"Let's carry these rolls on down while they're still fresh," responded her mother, "and you can see firsthand."

Ten minutes later, Emma Jane helped her mother carry the large box of dinner rolls into the sunny church fellowship hall. Dozens of people—retired men, teenagers, housewives, and working ladies on their lunch hour, some black, some white, some church members, and many whom Emma Jane had never seen before—seemed to be busy preparing a huge dinner. But there was no table set. Instead, the dinners were carefully being packed into individual plastic and foam containers.

"Mrs. Sullivan! Thank goodness for you and your ten dozen rolls," a cheerful voice called out. Emma Jane recognized Mrs. Farrell, their minister's vivacious young wife. Mrs. Farrell had their baby son, Daniel, strapped on her back in a blue denim pouch.

"I was happy to pick up the rolls," replied Emma Jane's mother. "It looks hectic today."

"It is absolutely wild," answered Mrs. Farrell. "We added 10 new guests to our delivery route, and the flu bug struck. We have 65 dinners to deliver to shut-ins and elderly folks and nobody to pack up silverware or wrap those delicious-looking rolls you brought."

"I can help," a quiet voice spoke.

It was Emma Jane. "I can do the silverware and the rolls," she nodded, "and maybe I could play with baby Daniel afterward, so that you can finish your work Mrs. Farrell."

"Are you sure?" her mother asked.

"Yes," answered Emma Jane. "I want to help people, and I want to find out more about the people who need to have their lunch brought to them. Don't they have families or food of their own?"

GP275702 Developing Character in Christian Kids

Emma Jane . . . continued

"Many elderly or sick people have little money to buy nutritious food," answered Mrs. Farrell, "or they might feel too sick or too weak to prepare their meals. Sometimes elderly folks become forgetful and don't remember to eat a good meal for days at a time."

"Are they all alone?" Emma Jane asked, with compassion in her voice.

"A lot of people are alone and very lonely, too," answered her mother. "But *Meals on Wheels* can help. The volunteers bring hot meals and a friendly visitor to check in on older citizens."

"I like this idea," agreed Emma Jane. "It reminds me of the parable in the Bible, where Jesus takes the five loaves of bread and a few fish and feeds the five thousand followers."

"That's a wonderful story," smiled Mrs. Farrell, and they began to work.

For several weeks that summer, Emma Jane spent Tuesday and Thursday afternoons helping with *Meals on Wheels*. She wrapped silverware, fixed tea jars, and watched baby Daniel. One day, Mrs. Farrell asked Emma Jane whether she would like to actually help deliver some meals.

"It is time for you to meet some of the wonderful folks who eat the meals," she smiled.

Emma Jane's eyes shone with excitement as the van pulled up in front of a quiet cottage on Laurel Lane. "Look at the tall grass and weeds in the yard," whispered Emma Jane. "It doesn't even look like anybody lives here."

Mrs. Farrell carefully lifted a boxed dinner from the back of the van, and they went up the walk. Knocking on the dusty front door, Mrs. Farrell called out, "Hello Mrs. Jenkins! Dinner is served."

"Come in, come in," called a frail but cheerful voice.

Propped on a worn print sofa was a tiny, yellow-looking old lady. Her hair was pulled back into a frizzed-looking gray bun, and her eyes looked tired. But Emma Jane did not have a chance to study the lady's face because her eyes were fixed on the beautiful embroidery on her dressing gown.

Emma Jane . . . continued

"What beautiful flowers!" exclaimed Emma Jane. She reached out to touch the silky threads, but suddenly remembered her manners.

"Don't be shy little girl," insisted Mrs. Jenkins. "I am happy to have some young, lively friends, especially someone who appreciates handiwork."

"I do," said Emma Jane. "I've never seen any embroidery like it."

"Well then, take a look at this," said the old lady, drawing a satin pillow from the pile behind her back. The pillow was designed with violet, blue, gold, and red flowers and hearts. Emma Jane admired the lovely patterns.

"We have your favorite chicken pot pie today," said Mrs. Farrell. "Best to eat up while it is still hot, and there is peach cobbler for dessert."

"Let me help you," offered Emma Jane. She helped the elderly lady sit up and settle the tray on her lap. She liked Mrs. Jenkins' friendly smile and bright blue eyes.

"It is a blessing to have such good friends," sighed Mrs. Jenkins. "You will understand that when you get old," she told Emma Jane.

"I am beginning to understand a lot of things," Emma Jane told her. "I would like to come back and see more of your beautiful work, and maybe my dad and I could do some work in your yard. Then you could go out on the porch and see something pretty."

"That would be marvelous!" Mrs. Jenkins clasped her small hands and smiled.

Emma Jane and Mrs. Farrell climbed back into the van. There were a lot more chicken pot pie dinners to deliver. "So much work to do," thought Emma Jane, "and I am ready to do it."

"One hundred and ten years ago, Jane Addams was doing work like this," Emma Jane told Mrs. Farrell as they drove to the next home.

"Yes, and Jesus was encouraging us to do it thousands of years earlier," agreed Mrs. Farrell.

"Some things never change, I guess," nodded Emma Jane, "if they are important enough." She pulled out the list. "Turn right at that stop sign Mrs. Farrell. We have a new guest to feed."

Emma Jane's Discovery

Language Arts

1. After reading the story aloud, instruct the children to write a letter to Miss Jane Addams at Hull House in Chicago. The children can describe why they would like a summer job working at Hull House. They should describe their motivation and the talents and abilities they have that they might share with others.

2. Divide the children into teams to create a "Word Web" with the word *compassion* in the center. Simply give the children 11" x 14" sheets of paper, markers, and thesauruses they can use to find as many words as they can that are similar to *compassion.* Post the word webs around the room.

3. Encourage children to read more biographies about men and women who showed compassion in their lives and work. Each time a child reads a biography, have him or her fill out a copy of activity page 72. Also, have the children give a report on their biographies.

4. Using the classified advertisement section of the newspaper, divide the children into teams of 4–5 and give each team the same section of the Sunday classified ads. You will need several sets. Write the following categories on a large sheet of posterboard:

   • Jobs that require skill

   • Jobs that require skill and compassion

   • Jobs that don't place great demands on a person

   Ask the teams to cut out ads for jobs that fill each category. Tape each team's selections under the categories. Discuss the results. Ask the children how they inferred the need for skill or compassion from what the ad said or from what they already know about the job.

5. Ask the children to imagine that they are older persons who receive a *Meals on Wheels* lunch each day. Then give each child a blank thank-you note and instruct the children to use their best handwriting to write "thank-you notes" to the workers who bring them lunch. Tell the children to include at least one reason why they appreciate the meal. It is not enough to say "thank you," though that is important. The purpose of this task is for the children to think through and write down why the ministry is valuable.

6. Have the children prepare menus of meals that they could prepare and give to people in need. The children should plan how to get the food, how to prepare and pack it, and how and to whom it should be delivered. Help the children enact their plan.

7. The children could hold a food drive. Let them use boxes to sort the food to give to those who need it. Have the children include Bible verses and prayers of hope in each box they prepare.

Emma Jane's Discovery

Social Studies

1. Encourage the children to invite an older relative or church member who is an immigrant to come for a class visit. Have the children ask this guest questions about the hardships and struggles involved in finding a home in a new country. The children can ask him or her to describe a favorite food or holiday from "the old country." Then give the children copies of page 73 to complete.

2. Create a bulletin board of "Compassionate Works in Contemporary Society." Ask the children to bring in clippings that show how compassion is still at work today in God's people.

3. Do an Internet search on *immigration.* Find out about new groups of immigrants coming to the United States today. Mark the countries of origin on a classroom world map. Ask the children to consider the challenges that these new immigrants might face today.

4. One reason that Jane Addams was so successful in social work was her understanding of different cultures. To develop the children's knowledge base, let them try solving "Geo-Riddles." Using a globe of the world and their social studies textbooks as references, help the children sharpen their geography skills by solving the riddles below. Make up additional riddles using your textbook and the globe to help the children remember important geography facts. Then let them create their own riddles.

   • I am a famous European city. I begin with a "P" and contain the Eiffel Tower and the Seine River. What am I? (Paris)

   • I cut the United States down the middle, and my rich delta ends in the city of New Orleans. What am I? (Mississippi River)

   • Dividing the earth into two hemispheres is hard work, especially when it is so hot! What am I? (equator)

   • I am the continent known for the Great Sphinx in the north and diamond mines in the south. What am I? (Africa)

5. Have the children research countries in which people are hungry. In groups, have them prepare reports detailing why people are hungry, what resources they lack, and suggestions of things that could be done to help the people.

6. Help the children learn about hunger in your society. Have them research various organizations that help feed the hungry. Compile a list of them and post copies of it around the church or school. The children could also make posters encouraging others to feed the hungry.

Emma Jane's Discovery

Character Building Enrichment

1. Set up a class visit to a *Meals on Wheels* or other similar ministry. After the tour, ask the children to consider how they can participate in a regular, meaningful way.

2. Divide the children into teams and have them research to find stories in which Jesus showed compassion to others. Give them copies of activity page 74 to complete. When the pages are completed, have each group present its page.

3. Tell the children that many immigrants flee their native countries because of religious persecution. Invite a local pastor or professor to come into the class to talk about the realities of Christians who are currently being persecuted for their faith around the globe, especially in Communist or Muslim countries. Give the children copies of page 75 to use to write answers to questions they ask. (Note: If individual children can each interview someone, reports could be written up and shared with the class.)

4. Talk with your local pastor or a missions-minded pastor about a foreign or local missions project that the children can assist with. Once you have decided on a small, specific project, use copies of page 76 to help the children brainstorm ways to help. For example, one group of children found that a missionary needed a bicycle to travel the congested streets of the inner city where he worked in Asia. The children collected and recycled soda cans to pay for this bicycle.

5. In the story, "Emma Jane's Discovery," the character recognizes an important truth about herself and about life. Give the children copies of page 77 to use to help them see how God uses situations and challenges to help each of us "discover" inner strengths and to help us discover how important it is to rely on God's wisdom and plan for our lives.

Name _____

Biography Book Talk

Title of the biography _____

Author _____

What did your subject accomplish in his or her life that made the world a better place? _____

_____

_____

_____

_____

How did your subject show a commitment to compassion in his or her life? _____

_____

_____

_____

_____

Did your subject have to overcome any obstacles in his or her life?

_____

_____

_____

_____

After reading this biography, would you like to be like this person? Why or why not? _____

_____

_____

_____

_____

Name _____

Post Card From the Old Country

After talking with your older visitor about his or her experiences living in a foreign country, send a "post card" to him or her pretending you are visiting that country. Describe what you learned about the country and thank him or her for visiting your class. You might draw and write about a food, scene, or celebration that interested you on your visit on the "front" (top) of the card.

Dear _____,

_____

_____

_____   To: _____

_____   _____

_____   _____

_____   From: _____

_____   _____

    Sincerely,   _____

_____

Jesus the Compassionate Savior

Fill out the chart below, showing 2–3 examples of situations in which Jesus showed compassion to others. Be specific. You may work in pairs or teams to complete this activity.

Situation One _____

_____

_____

Location in Bible _____

_____

_____

Situation Two _____

_____

_____

Location in Bible _____

_____

_____

Situation Three _____

_____

_____

Location in Bible _____

_____

_____

Name _____

Christians Under Persecution

Organize your interview with a pastor, professor, or missionary who knows about the persecution of Christians in other countries by completing the questions below.

Interviewer or Team _____

Date _____ Interviewee _____

Questions:

1. What kind of persecution are Christians dealing with in other countries? _____

_____

_____

2. Can you show us on a globe or map the countries in which Christians are persecuted for their faith? These countries are _____

_____.

3. Do the laws in these countries allow persecution because of religion? _____ How is that different from the United States? _____

_____

_____

4. How can we help Christians who are not allowed to worship freely?

_____

_____

_____

5. Does the persecution seem to stop Christians from living their faith? _____ Are many people still being saved? _____

_____

_____

Name _____

Missions on My Mind

This page is the perfect way to organize your class plan for a mission project.

Mission Team Members: _____

Teacher: _____

Our missionaries live and work in _____

_____.

They are trying to _____

_____.

We found out that our mission friends need _____

_____.

They need these things to _____

_____.

We want to accomplish the following in order to help:

1. _____

2. _____

We will raise money for the items by _____

_____,

or we can gather the items by _____

_____.

We can get these things to our mission friends by____

_____.

Our target date to finish this project is _____.

Discovering Characters in the Bible

Complete this activity page using your Bible and dictionary as reference tools. Your task is to figure out what each character "discovered" about his or her personal character through his or her experiences.

Part One

Use your dictionary to write the definition of the word *discovery*.

_____

_____

Do you think that a discovery that you make about yourself is the same as discovering a planet or a cure for cancer? Explain.

_____

_____

_____

_____

Part Two

Read about the characters listed below in the Bible. What do you think they "discovered" about how they thought or behaved?

John the Baptist _____

Jonah _____

Mary Magdalene_____

Moses _____

Mary _____

Sarah _____

Ruth _____

Barabbas _____

Dear Parents,

Teaching character is an important part of Christian education, and one of our most natural methods is the use of stories. Stories found in a book entitled, *Developing Character in Christian Kids*, show children in real-life situations, learning how character really counts. Making decisions, taking responsibility for their actions, working hard, respecting elders, caring for pets, sharing resources, improving the community, recognizing the value of differences among people—all of these situations help children to grow and develop spiritually, and all are featured in this book.

In addition to reading the stories described above, our class will complete a number of academic lessons that build on the themes from each story. In language arts, social studies, science, geography, math, and the arts, we take the important themes from the stories and reinforce basic academic and critical thinking skills.

Sometimes, we invite parents and community friends to be part of the lessons. You may be asked to share your family history, your political views, your career path, or some other aspect with the children. We value your experiences and ideas.

Please feel free to ask for copies of the stories to share at home. We want the entire family to enjoy these stories and to work together with the school in *Developing Character in Christian Kids*.

Yours truly,

Ideas for Building Community Support

- Develop a "Character Counts" award that your school can award annually to a community member who demonstrates the core values.

- Give the children in your school regular opportunities to work on community-wide projects.

- Adopt a nursing home and make regular visits to the patients.

- Donate food to an SPCA animal shelter.

- Lobby your local school board to place character education in the public school curriculum.

- Display children's artwork in the community.

- Involve the children in making the school and church grounds attractive and neat.

- Take steps to make sure that biographies about individuals with good character are part of your school and community libraries.

- Start a scout troop or other service organization at your school.

- Invite local "experts" from colleges or counseling centers to present workshops on character education issues. Invite school and community members to attend.

Appendix

Checklist for Character Education

This assessment tool can be used as an insert to the regular report card, or it can serve as an evaluation tool for materials saved in a Character Education portfolio.

Student _____   Evaluation Period _____

Character Trait	Rating Scale			Comments
	Strong Commitment 3	2	Needs Improvement 1	
Demonstrates a strong work ethic				
Respects individual differences				
Shows kindness to others				
Demonstrates the qualities of a good citizen and servant				
Reflects personal responsibility				
Shows compassion				

GP275702 Developing Character in Christian Kids